ESTATE PUBLICATIONS

GRIMSBY · CLEETHORP[ES]
IMMINGHAM · LACEBY · WALTHAM

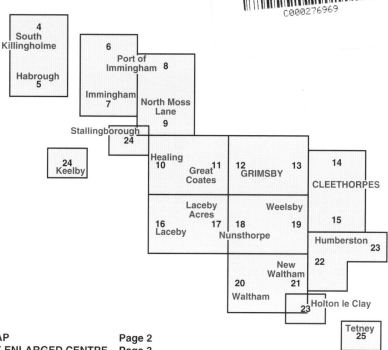

ROAD MAP	Page 2
GRIMSBY ENLARGED CENTRE	Page 3
INDEX TO STREETS	Page 25

Scale of street plans: 4 Inches to 1 Mile (unless otherwise stated)

▬▬	Motorway
▬▬	'A' Road / Dual
▬▬	'B' Road / Dual
▬▬	Minor Road / Dual
▬▬	Track
▨▨	Pedestrianized
—■—	Railway / Station
- - -	Footpath

Every effort has been made to verify the accuracy of information in this book but the publishers cannot accept responsibility for expense or loss caused by an error or omission. Information that will be of assistance to the user of the maps will be welcomed.

The representation on these maps of a road, track or path is no evidence of the existence of a right of way.

～	Stream / River
～Lock	Canal
→	One-way Street
P	Car Park
C	Public Convenience
i	Tourist Information
+	Place of Worship
●	Post Office

[Str]eet plans prepared and published by ESTATE PUBLICATIONS, Bridewell House, TENTERDEN, KENT. The Publishers acknowledge the co-operation of the local authorities of towns represented in this atlas.

Ordnance Survey® This product includes mapping data licensed from Ordnance Survey® with the permission of the Controller of Her Majesty's Stationery Office.

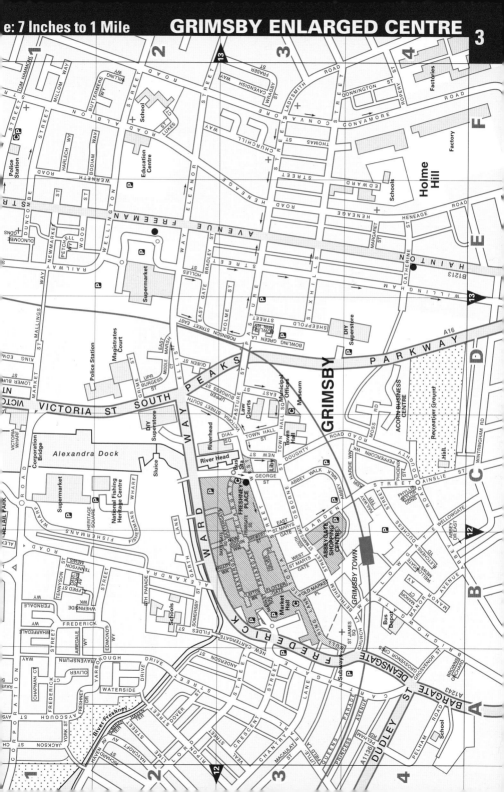

North Killingholme

South Killingholme

Flare Stack

HUMBER REFINERY

Walmer House

Main Gate

Works

Works

Works

OIL REFINERIES

Fire Station

Moat

Manor Farm

Village Hall

Hotel

Vicarage Farm

Westfield Farm

Community Centre

St DENYS CL

MOAT LANE

STAPLE LANE

FARBEN VILLAS

BRIAR CL

PILGRIMS CL

Sch

MAYFLOWER

GREENGATE

HAWKINS WY

SCHOOL RD

Manor Farm

Holton Farm

Primitive Chapel La

Baptist La

Mayfield Av

Woods La

The Poplars

Warehouses

INDUSTRIAL ESTATE

Airfield (disused)

EAST FIELD ROAD

EAST FIELD ROAD

HALTON ROAD TOP

MIDDLE WEST

MERE ROAD

A160

HUMBER ROAD

ROAD STREET

EAST FIELD ROAD

STREET

A160 ROAD

CHURCH LANE

VICARAGE LANE

NICHOLSON LANE

St CRISPINS CL

CLARKES RD

APPROACH

LANCASTER

TOWN

HABROUGH

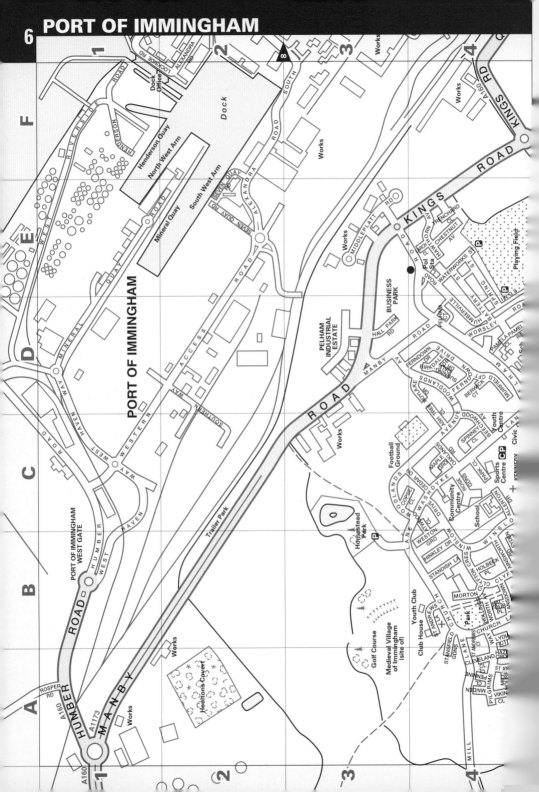

Immingham

Mauxhall Farm

Community Centre

Museum & Resource Centre

Playing Field

Highfield Farm

School

Swim Pool

Surgery

Sports Grnd

School

Highfield

STALLINGBOROUGH

HABROUGH ROAD

A1173

A180

B1210 ROAD

SOUTH MARSH ROAD INDUSTRIAL ESTATE

POWER STATION

SOUTH MARSH ROAD

MARSH ROAD

Wadd Farm

A180

Oldfleet Drain

Middle Drain

SOUTH LANE

Poplar Farm

ROAD

MARSH

Primrose Cottage

Meadows Farm

Mead Cottages

MOSS LANE

Eleanor House

SOUTH LANE

CARR LANE

ROAD

NORTH MOSS LANE INDUSTRIAL ESTATE

BEELSBOURNE ROAD

NORTH

KILN

WEIHEIM WY

Fire Station

KILN LANE

EPHAMS LANE

A1173

MANOR CT

ALMOND GRO

HUNSLEY DR

STATION

School

BUTTERCROSS CL

CLARKSON DR

PARKSD

B

GARSC

CARSC

STALLABOROUGH

HOLLY

THE WOODLANDS

Fire Station

A180

HUNSLEY DR

School

Oldfleet Drain

HEALING

Rec Grnd

Mea...
Fa...

Meadow
Cottages

ASHLEIGH CT

Sports
Ground

STALLINGBOROUGH ROAD

B1210

WESTWOOD

POPLAR

HAWTHORN CL

LUCAS CT

ROWAN DR

ROAD

OAK

AVENUE

AVENUE

Sch

BEVERLEY CT

NICHOLSON ROAD

MEADOW DR

PINE WK

CHESTNUT WK

ROAD

DRIVE

BUTTERCUP CT

WISTERIA

BURDERA CL

LARKSPUR

BLUEBELL

FORSYTHIA AV

CLADING CT

AV

CLEMATIS

APPLE TREE CT

CORNFLOWER CL

SNOWDROP CL

COWSLIP

MALLARD CT

SWALLOW CT

PRIMROSE

BRIAR

ROOKERY RD

CARLTON

CARLTON

LANE

AVENUE

RD

STATION

LOW RD

THE

MCLEIGH CT

FORDS

RADCLIFFE

Rec Grnd

MAPLE GRO

LINDSEY

ELM GRO

NICHOLSON DRIVE

Manor Farm

WELLS

GREAT ROAD

IVY FARM CT

ANNEX

School

Healing

COATES

LANE

CARR LANE

Meadow
Farm

The Manor

Moat

AYLESBY

Mount
Pleasant

Maud Hole
Covert

Wybers

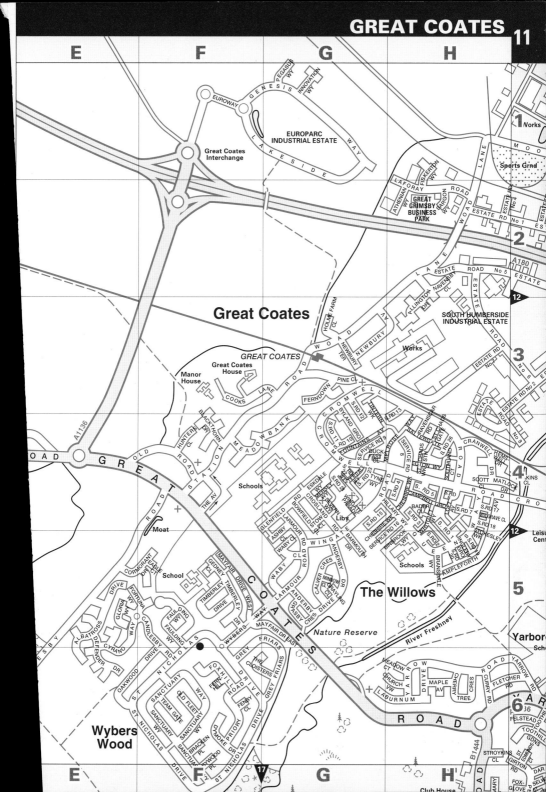

E   **F**   **G**   **H**

EUROWAY

PEGASUS WY
GENESIS WY
INNOVATION WY
LAKESIDE WAY

EUROPARC INDUSTRIAL ESTATE

Great Coates Interchange

Works

MOO

Sports Grnd

LAFORAY
ATHENIAN
FISKERTON WY
WAGON

GREAT GRIMSBY BUSINESS PARK

ROAD

ESTATE RD No 4
ESTATE RD No 1
ESTATE

A180

ROAD No 5
ESTATE ROAD
ALLINGTON AV
NAVENBY CL
NEWBURY AV

Great Coates

12

SOUTH HUMBERSIDE INDUSTRIAL ESTATE

GREAT COATES

Great Coates House

Manor House

COOKS LANE

WORCESTER ROAD
HOLME FARM CL
NEWBURY

Works

ESTATE RD No 6
ESTATE RD No 8

3

PINE CL
FERNDOWN
CROMWELL WK

CROMWELL ROAD
S.RD 12
S.RD 13
S RD 11
BYLAND GRO
COUNTAINS
ESKDALE RD
CROSLAND
S RD 14
S RD 20
TYNE WY
BUCK FAST
RAVENSPAR
EGTON WY
CRANWELL
HEMS WR

12

BLACKTHORN DR
HUNTERS CL
STATION ROAD
THE AV
MEADOWBANK

Schools

GLENFIELD RD
ASHBY
WABY CL
LARMOUR RD
BOWFIELD RD
CROSLAND
WEST
Liby
WINGATE
S.RD 15
S RD 21
SERVICE RD
HILLARY
CAMPBELL
BADER
SCOTT
GROVE CL
S.RD 5
S.RD 1
S RD 17
MATLOCK
ROYD
KINS CL

4

Moat

CLAD
WABY
WINGATE ROAD
ANDERBY
BARMOUTH
CHESHIRE WY
SERVICE RD 16
LINBROOK WY
KINGSMEAD WY
BRANSDALE
AMPLEFORTH
S.RD 18
ANNESLEY
STONESLEY

12

Leisu Cent

CORMORANT DR
EAGLE DR
School
FORTUNA WY
GLORIA WY
ALBATROSS DR
DEFENDER DR
CYRANO DR
CANDLESBY RD
MAYFAIR DRIVE WEST
GECKNE
TIMBERLEY CL
TIMBERLEY DRIVE
FAULDING WY
FAULDINGLAS
WYBERS WY
MAYFAIR DR EAST
LARMOUR RD
WABY
ANDERBY
FRASBY
CALVER CRES
MINNOW DR
GRAYLING CRES
ANDERBY DRIVE

Schools

The Willows

5

OAKWOOD ST
NICH ST
SANCTUARY ST
OLD FLEET
TEAM GATE
SANCTUARY WY
SANCTUARY PL
FERN
FOXHILL DR
HAYWOOD DR
DYMOKE PRIORY DR
ST NICHOLAS DRIVE
FENBY CL
GREY FRIARS
THE CLOISTERS
FRIARS
PRIORY ROAD
GREY FRIARS DRIVE

Nature Reserve

River Freshney

Yarbor Sch

MEADOW CT
CHURCH YARROW DRIVE
LABURNUM
CHURCH AV
MAPLE AV
CHERRY TREE
CURRY RD
CRES
FLETCHER RD
YARROW RD

Wybers Wood

17

R O A D

B1444

STROYKINS CL
FELSTEAD RD
TOOTHILL
GOIS
GIRTON
FOX GLOVE

6
36

Club House

E   **F**   **G**   **H**

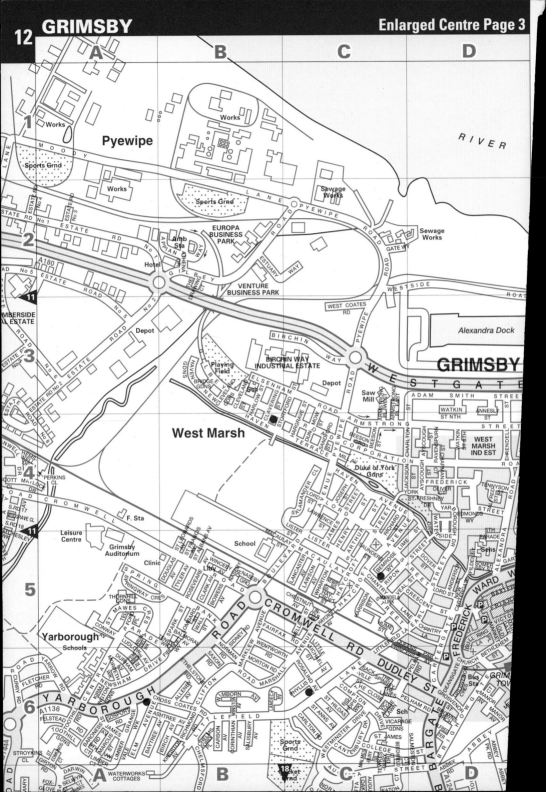

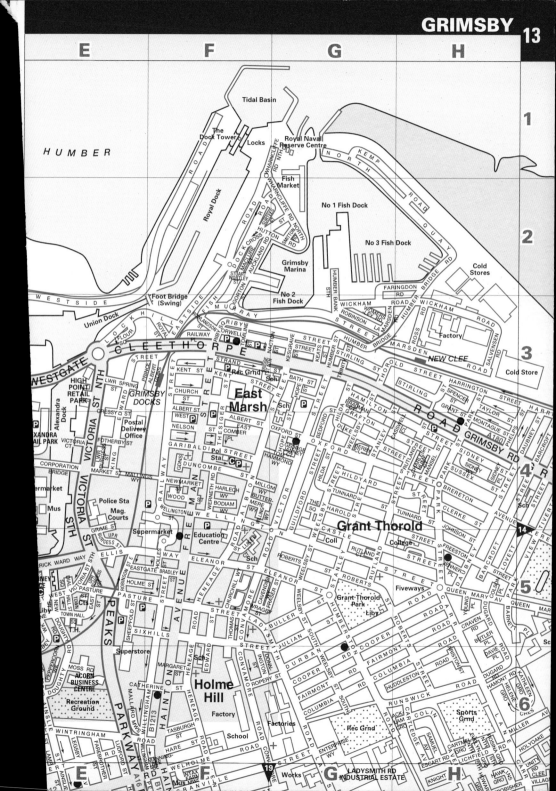

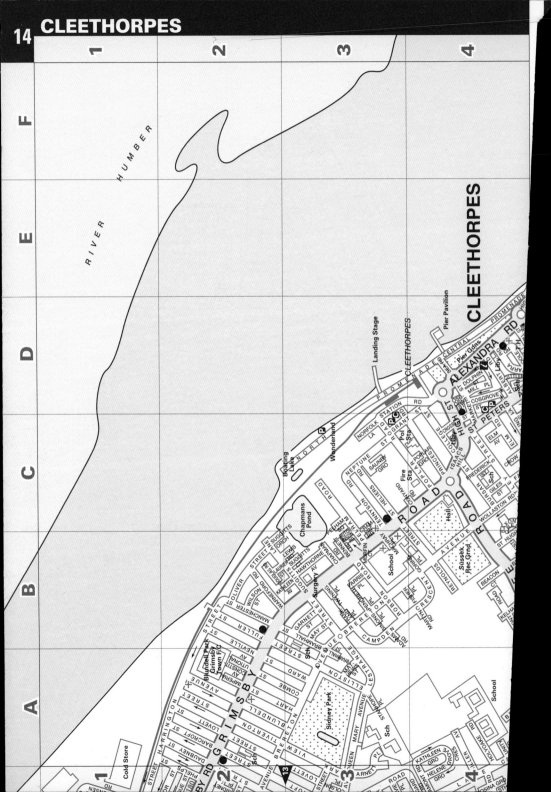

RIVER HUMBER

CLEETHORPES

Pier Pavilion

Landing Stage

Pier Gdns

ALEXANDRA RD

PETERS

PROMENADE

CLEETHORPES

HIGH ST

COLLEGE

PROMENADE

NORFOLK LA

STATION RD

Pol Sta

GRANT ST

POPLAR

Wonderland

Boating Lake

NORTH

ROAD

Fire Sta

NEPTUNE

SAUNBY GRO

ST HELIERS

TENNYSON

Chapmans Pond

SUGGITTS

SUGGITTS

LEWS

STREET

OLIVER ST

WILSON RD

MANCHESTER ST

WARNEFORD RD

KATHLEEN

HAWTHORNE

Surgery

CHAPMAN AV

School

Hall

Sussex Rec Grnd

AVENUE

REYNOLDS

BEACON

Blundell Park
Grimsby
Town FC

FULLER ST

NEVILLE ST

COMBE ST

HART ST

BLUNDELL ST

TIVERTON ST

BRERETON AV

VIEW

GARNETT ST

BRAMHALL

MAY ST

WARD

STREET

GRANGE

CAMPDEN

ELLISTON

STANLEY

MARY AVENUE

Sidney Park

Sch

School

Cold Store

GRIMSBY RD

HARRINGTON ST

LOVETT ST

BARCROFT ST

DAUNBEY ST

PHELPS ST

AVENUE

A **B** **10** **C** **D**

1

Pyewipe Farm

2

Aylesby

MEMORIAL COTTAGES

AYLESBY RD

AYLESBY

3

BUTT

Little Beck

BUTT LANE

BLYTH WAY

LANE

LANE

Playing Field

Little Beck

Laceby Beck

ARNOLD CL

BURLEY CL

HARNEIS CRES

Nursing Home

Sewage Works

GIBRALTAR LA

BRRY RD

BUTT LANE

LONGMEADOWS DR

ANFORD CL

4

COOPER

Recreation Ground

School

BUTTERBEL CL

SEED CLOSE

AUSTIN GARTH LA

PHILLIPS LA

Little Laceby

THE MEAD

IIBY

LANE

NEW CHAPEL LA

OLD CHAPEL LA

Laceby

St FRANCIS GRO

Cemy

CEMETERY CRES

BROOKS CL

Comm Centre

HIGH ST

FIELD

CHURCH LA

ROAD

ST PETERS GRO

KEITH

CHARLES

CEMETERY

KNIGHTS CL

ALTOFT RD

ROAD

SPRING LA

GRIMSBY

GEORGE BUTLER CL

5

ST MARGARETS LA

CRESCENT

KENMAR

AVENUE

SNOW MWS

ROAD

P

Youth Centre

WHITGIFT CL

GRANGE AV

TREVOR

NEW

The Limes Farm

FIELD HEAD LA

YEWS LA

ELM LA

BREEDON RD

CAISTOR RD

Clinic

WILLOW CL

CAISTOR

GRIMSBY

ROAD

A18

A46

6

LOPHAM LANE

New Farm

ROAD

A **B** **C** **D**

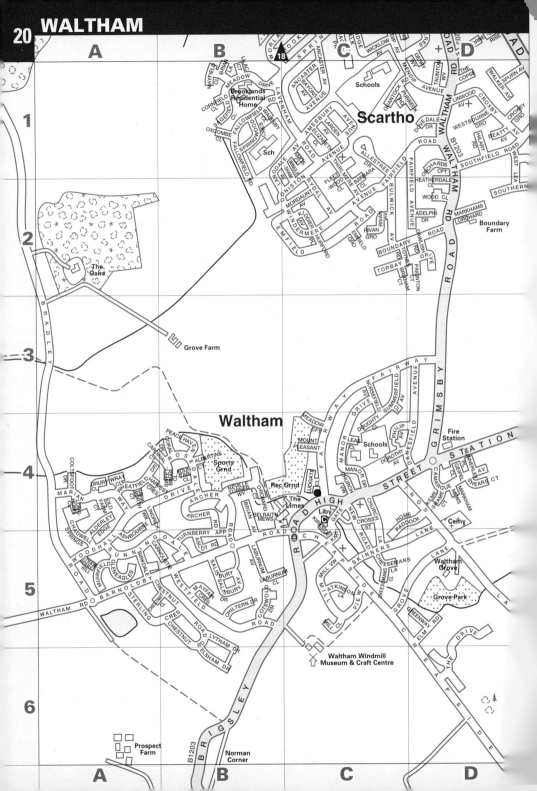

Scartho

Waltham

The Gairs

Grove Farm

Schools

Boundary Farm

Fire Station

Sports Grnd

Rec Grnd

The Limes

Library

Home Paddock

Cemy

Waltham Grove

Grove Park

Prospect Farm

Norman Corner

Waltham Windmill Museum & Craft Centre

Brooklands Residential Home

A B 15 C D

A

HEWITTS AV
ALTYRE WY
Superstore
BUSINESS PARK
Peaks Covert Farm
A16
19

WILTON RD
JACKSONS
BRADLEY CNR
PLACE

WILTON ROAD INDUSTRIAL ESTATE

GRIMSBY ROAD

ROAD

WINDERMERE CRES
DERWENT DRIVE
CONISTON
GRASMERE GRO
LOMOND GRO
BUTTERMERE CRES
CRESCENT

B

WF
CHAFINCH
GREENFINCH WAY
ROSEMARY
BECKSIDE CL
BULLFINCH
BECK
BROUGHTON DR
HONEYSUCKLE
PRIMROSE
MARLBOROUGH WAY
BRAMBLE CL
HAMPTON CL
CRANB CL
CRANBOURNE

CHELTENHAM
GOODWOOD
KEMPTON
AYLING MERE
DELAMERE CTS
COTTS

WESTPORT RD
WALDORF
MEADOW RD
HALL
MAYFAIR CT
WESTBURY
RD

FAIRGATE
LITTLE BECK

HUMBERSTON RD
NORTH SEA LA
SOUTH VW

ENNER DALE CL
LOMOND GRO
QUEEN ELIZABETH RD
ST PETERS RD
QUEEN ELIZABETH
PAUL CRES
ST CROFTS RD
CHIPPENDALE CL
SHERATON CL

ST CHRISTOPHERS
ST JOHNS CRES
ST STEPHEN CRES
ST LUKES CRES
ST MARKS RD
ST MATTHEWS
ROAD
ST THOMAS CL
CRES
MIDFIEL
THE

Golf Course
Schools

CHURCH AVENUE

THE
Lib'y
CHUR

The Humberston Country Club

3

AVENUE

BARN DR
QUERIM DR
ASPHODEL CL
TAMAR DR
PARK

GLEBE RD
THE ELMS
GLEBE
LONSDALE CL
Sch
ADLARD GRO
LIME GRO
ROAD
Man Far

TETNEY

ABBOTTS GRANGE

4
B1219
AV HUMBERSTON
CANON OAKES
Scout Camp
Club House
21

HUMBERSTON AVENUE

Cemy

WALK LANE
SOUTH S
LA
COTTAGE YARD LA

Kirby Farm

Humberston Park
Golf Course

5

O

ROAD

6

A B C D

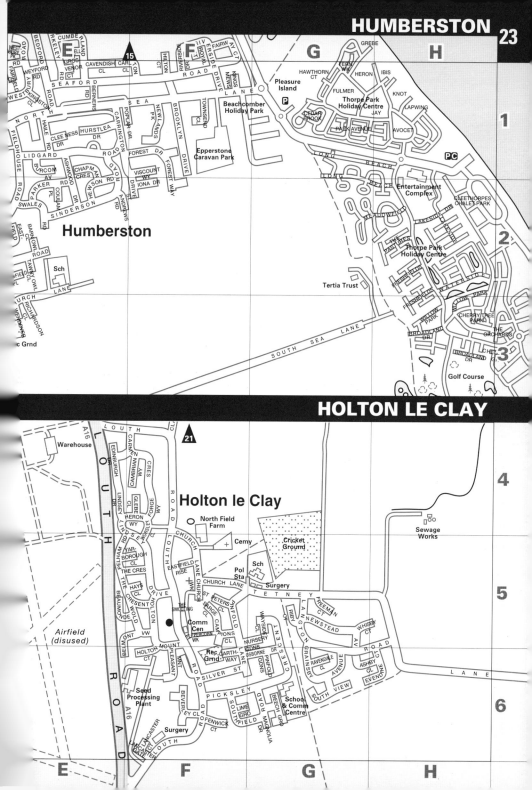

HOLTON LE CLAY

Humberston

Holton le Clay

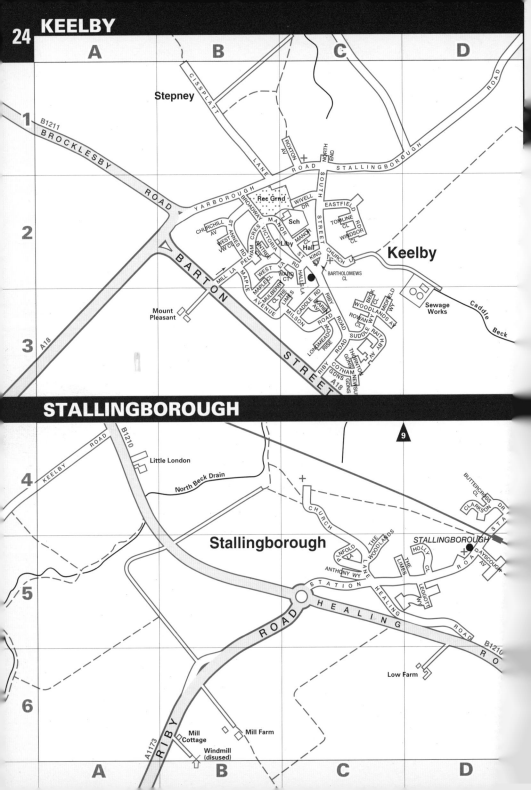

KEELBY

A   B   C   D

1

B1211
BROCKLESBY ROAD
Stepney
CISSPLATT LANE
ROXTON AV
NORTH END
ROAD
SOUTH STREET
STALLINGBOROUGH

2

A18
BARTON STREET
YARBOROUGH
BROADWAY
CHURCHILL AV
ST ANNES RD
VW CL
MILL LA
MAPLE
WEST WD
MAPLE CL
PELHAM GRES
ANTHE
VICTORIA
MANOR DR
Rec Grnd
Sch
Liby
Hall
MANOR CL
KING ST
WIVELL DR
EASTFIELD
TOMLINE CL
WINDSOR CL
CHURCH
Keelby
BARTHOLEMEWS CL
BECK
WOODLANDS WY
MIDFIELD WY
Sewage Works
Caddle Beck

3

A18
Mount Pleasant
MULBERRY CL
THE LIMES
HALL LA
CADDLE RD
RIBY RD
LONGMEADOW RISE
MILSON
RIBY ROAD
ROWANS
SUDDLE
RAITHBY AV
THORNTON GDNS
COTHAM GDNS
NEWSUM GDNS
CADDLE RD

STALLINGBOROUGH

▲ 9

4

KEELBY ROAD
B1210
Little London
North Beck Drain
CHURCH LANE
BUTTERCROSS CL
CLARKSON
STA

5

Stallingborough
NFOLD LA
ANTHONY WY
THE WOODLANDS
THE LIMES
HOLLY CL
STALLINGBOROUGH
DAYSCOUGH
AV
LEGGOTT WY
STATION ROAD
HEALING
ROAD
HEALING
ROAD
B1210 RO

6

A1173
RIBY ROAD
Mill Cottage
Mill Farm
Windmill (disused)
Low Farm

A   B   C   D